Glasgow University Publications

THE CURIOUS DIVERSITY

THE CURIOUS DIVERSITY

Glasgow University on Gilmorehill:
The First Hundred Years

UNIVERSITY OF GLASGOW
1970

Printed in Great Britain by Robert MacLehose and Company Ltd.
The University Press, Glasgow

Foreword

. . . of explanation. This is not a formal history of the University of Glasgow during the last hundred years on Gilmorehill: nor is it a progress report: nor, indeed, a report of any kind. It is, rather, a scrap-book, an anecdotal rescue operation. It is, moreover, the very small tip of a very large iceberg of fact and fable that has accumulated in the century since 1870.

The idea of preserving some of it before it melted away originated with the student members of the Centenary Committee, with, in particular, Anthony Cassidy who, with Alison Middleton and Elizabeth Meldrum of the Publications Office, has carried out the research and editing. The sources exploited include those of the *Glasgow University Magazine*, the *College Courant*, assorted newspaper files, the volumes of press cuttings about the University preserved by the University, and the patience and memory of Mr C. A. Oakley. And if any of it should prove memorable, then under the terms of one light hearted definition it IS history.

Acknowledgements

Photographs nos. 58, 60, 61, 62, 63, 63a, 67, 68, 77, 78, 79, 83, 84, 86, 87, 88, 91 and 92 are reproduced by courtesy of the *Glasgow Herald*.

Photographs nos. 1 and 2 are reproduced by courtesy of Messrs T. and R. Annan and Sons, Ltd.

Names

Reader, observe the curious diversity
Of names which signify the University.
The embryonic, skull-capped "loonie",
Nick-names that stately pile, the "Unie".
Ad nauseam – (to make you ill) –
The *News* alludes to "Gilmorehill".
The pale-be-windowed youth, exuding knowledge,
Can't understand unless you call it "College".
A taste in ties, and cerebellar sparsity,
Go with a penchant for the title "Varsity".
The sporting man, so vocable and gay,
Will call it (minus swear-words) – "Up the way".
The chronic, with his apathetic crawl,
Declines to talk about the place at all.

The Squid (O. H. Mavor)

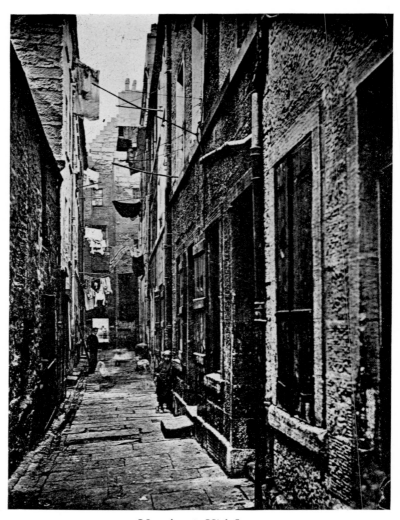

Vennel at 65 High Street

1870-1880

ZION OF THE WEST

"THE College of Glasgow is situated in an old and decayed part of the city where the very poorest of the population reside and where, as is usual in such localities, there is a very large number of whisky shops, little pawns, and houses in which disreputable persons of both sexes are harboured. The district is one of the worst of the city, as to the character of the inhabitants. Crimes and disorders are of daily occurrence, rendering it one of the most troublesome parts of the city to the police.

"From the character of the district altogether, it appears to me an unfit place for a great educational institution such as the University."

WHEN he condemned in these terms the site in the High Street of Glasgow occupied by the University, James Smart, Superintendent of Police, bore out the misgivings of members of the University itself. Before a Select Committee of the House of Lords fourteen years before, Dr Duncan Macfarlan, Principal of the University, had deplored, in the interests of staff and students alike, the environment of the college.

Was it, he was asked, in his opinion inconvenient and improper for the students? "I certainly think such exhibitions as they must witness," he answered, "and such language as must meet their ears almost continually in passing along these streets, are extremely injurious to their feelings, their tastes, and their morals."

AND so the University entered upon the immense undertaking of moving lock, stock, and barrel; classrooms, library, museum, equipment, books, collections of pictures and antiquities, professors and

Old College –
Inner Court

their households, and students; and of commissioning a new building on a new site. The site chosen was on the lands of Gilmorehill, on, according to a *Guide to Glasgow* of 1871, "a kind of teetotal Creemorne gardens."

It was beautiful, if less healthful than was hoped, being exposed to the city's prevailing soot-laden wind. Included in the purchase of it was the low-lying ground on the opposite bank of the River Kelvin. Since this was surplus to the University's requirements and the University needed money, Glasgow Town Council agreed to buy the ground and preserve it as park land. That there was a tinge of distrust of the University about this altruistic gesture emerged during a council meeting in October 1866:

"The acquisition will preserve the Park", it was reported, "from being spoiled by the erection of dwellings of an inferior class which might be the case supposing the authorities of the University should retain this portion of their purchase in their own hands. It would matter

Gilmorehill in the early nineteenth century

little to these authorities what sort of buildings were erected, because their own fine temple would stand above and overlook them into the West End palaces that skirt the brow of the opposite hill."

THE choice of an architect presented serious problems. The *Glasgow Herald* had taken upon itself to promise that "the new College, when built, will be one of the finest architectural ornaments of Glasgow". The task of designing the ornament fell to Mr George Gilbert Scott. "The preference which prevailed for the Gothic style", according to Professor Allen Thomson, chairman of the Building Committee, made the choice virtually inevitable. It sorely displeased Alexander "Greek" Thomson who had already been defeated by Scott in the competition for the design of the Albert Memorial and who disliked Gothic architecture in general and Scott-ish Gothic in particular.

Scott himself explained his design in these terms: "I adopted a style which I may call my own invention, having already initiated it in the

Sir George Gilbert Scott

Albert Institute at Dundee. It is simply a thirteenth or fourteenth-century secular style with the addition of certain Scottish features peculiar in that country to the sixteenth century, though in reality derived from the French style of the thirteenth and fourteenth centuries".

THE raising of funds was set in train for it had become clear at an early stage that the University's own resources would be insufficient to carry out Mr Scott's designs. A Joint Committee of "gentlemen unconnected with the University" was appointed to co-operate with the University authorities in raising money and within a remarkably short time of their appointment in May 1865, they had raised the sum of £82,450 from 150 subscriptions.

The Government – the Prime Minister, the Earl of Derby, was a former Rector – was reminded of its obligations to the University, of the fact that despite the great increase in the number of professorships and the consequent rise in expenditure, the University had received no assistance from public funds for more than two centuries. Government agreement to match the amount raised by subscription encouraged an immediate assault on the pockets of the citizens of Glasgow and the members of the General Council.

ALEXANDER THOMSON'S DESIGN FOR THE NATURAL HISTORY MUSEUM, SOUTH KENSINGTON

It has often wrongly been said that Thomson submitted a design for Glasgow University. The late William Power may have, unintentionally, been responsible for this. In an essay on Thomson in The World Unvisited, Glasgow, 1922, be reproduced a drawing of a domed building, faintly reminiscent of a St. Paul's Cathedral with flanking accretions which, he suggested, showed the University "as it might have been"; though be stated quite plainly that this architectural extravaganza was of his own devising, the unwary may have taken it for Thomson's. The above illustration, from an unexecuted design in the Mitchell Library, Glasgow, though intended for a building of a different purpose and on a very different site, gives a more authentic idea of what the University might have looked like had Thomson been responsible for it.

13

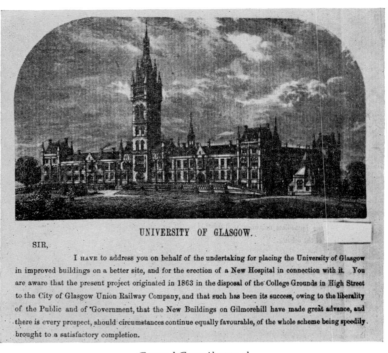

UNIVERSITY OF GLASGOW.

SIR,

      I HAVE to address you on behalf of the undertaking for placing the University of Glasgow in improved buildings on a better site, and for the erection of a New Hospital in connection with it. You are aware that the present project originated in 1863 in the disposal of the College Grounds in High Street to the City of Glasgow Union Railway Company, and that such has been its success, owing to the liberality of the Public and of Government, that the New Buildings on Gilmorehill have made great advance, and there is every prospect, should circumstances continue equally favourable, of the whole scheme being speedily brought to a satisfactory completion.

General Council appeal

BUILDING began. On June 6th 1866 the first sod was turned. Work went well – until the following spring. In April 1867, the masons employed on the site went on strike. It was a closed shop dispute which lasted until the autumn of 1868 during which time building was carried on by non-union labour.

On October 8th 1868, the foundation stones – there were two – were laid by the Prince and Princess of Wales. The *Glasgow Herald*, again in a prophetic mood, predicted for the day "an imposing spectacle". And indeed it was, as well as a lively one, for a nervous engineman caused the stone allotted to the Prince of Wales to rise jauntily into the air rather than sink gracefully into its place; and the Glasgow Choral Union could not at a slightly later point in the proceedings be prevailed upon to stop singing the Hallelujah Chorus.

By the autumn of 1870, the new buildings were ready. The pleasing

Floral archway at Kelvingrove,
October 1868

Archway near Pearce Lodge,
October 1868

15

*Gilmorehill
House*

*Foundation
stones of the new
building*

Laying of the foundation stones in October 1868

prospect inspired R.A.S. (Robert A. Sinclair) to write a fourteen verse eulogy for the *North British Daily Mail.*

"Ye walls that massive rise on Gilmorehill,
 With stately tower and many a turret crowned,
 Soon shall the thronging youth thy precincts fill,
 Soon render thine environs classic ground."

Verse fourteen hailed the University as "Joy of her children, Zion of the West!"

Senate leaving the Old College

Senate on the Lion and Unicorn Staircase in 1950

On November 7th, the University took possession and on the evening of the same day a celebration banquet was held in the Corporation Galleries at which the speeches were numerous, designed to inspire, and long. "The company separated", according to *The Scotsman* report, "at a late hour".

The departure from the Old College was commemorated in the famous photograph of the Senate on the Lion and Unicorn staircase. (The exercise was repeated eighty years later for the Fifth Centenary celebrations in 1951.)

RESURGAT IN GLORIA ALMA MATER

PASSING THE LOVING CUP AT UNIVERSITY DINNERS

The loving cup in use

a. Where the devil's that napkin?

b. Heavens—it tastes like cider!

c. I never can memorise those confounded words.

d. I'm sure this is all terribly unhygienic.

THE move from the High Street to Gilmorehill gave rise, however, to one of the as yet unsolved mysteries of the University. The Old College, it is known, possessed a collection of silver probably comparable to that of other ancient foundations of the same kind. During the earlier years of the University, students graduating were encouraged to present a gift of silver to the College. But for reasons that have never been explained, the University arrived in its new home with no more than a fraction of, presumably, a considerable collection. One loving cup, three candlesticks, and two "tasse" survived the journey.

THE silver was not, perhaps, the only casualty of the move. Something more intangible may have been lost, for with the removal to the west the close relationship between Town and Gown was weakened.

"There is little doubt that Glasgow gave up something of the old intimacy between Town and Gown when it moved west," one member of the senate later reflected. "It was of advantage to both Professors and

Foulis Academy of Arts Exhibition in the Inner Quadrangle of the Old College in 1761

South Front, c. 1880

merchants daily to rub shoulders on the 'plainstanes' of the Trongate, or
to sit down to dinner or supper at each other's board, or even on
occasion to enjoy a 'meridian' at the Saracen's Head or some other
popular hostelry or tavern."

MORE materially, during the first year on Gilmorehill, the students
complained of cold.

"We have heard much lately of the 'grandeur', 'magnificence', and
'stateliness' of the pile on Gilmorehill," one complained in a letter to
the *Glasgow Herald*", "but we have heard no expression indicative of
comfort which would have been more to the purpose so far as we are
concerned.

"The thing complained of most bitterly is the exceeding *coldness* of
the rooms. . . . The general reading room is so cold that unless one gets
near the fire – which, by-the-by, is no easy matter – he has to sit wrapped
up, just as one requires to be in such weather out of doors." There was
no convenient eating place, he went on, and no smoking salon.

"I very bitterly regret", one of his companions wrote in the same columns, "that I did not follow the example of my friends and leave the University, but I never expected we would have been so badly treated in Gilmorehill. I sigh," this medical student lamented, "when I am sitting hungry and cold in some of the class rooms to think of the comforts of High Street."

At the period of the removal to Gilmorehill, the University's curricula still concentrated on the Humanities, Philosophy, and Divinity. The planning of the new buildings reflected this emphasis and the Dean of the Faculty of Arts, Professor Hugh Blackburn, regarded a professor's needs as more than adequately satisfied by provision of a lecture room, a chair, a retiring room for the professor, and a few minor pieces of equipment such as a blackboard and chalk.

The study of law, medicine, and certain branches of science was carried out but under difficulties. Professor William Thomson (later Lord Kelvin) was grudgingly granted laboratory facilities. And although Professor Allen Thomson of the chair of Anatomy was chairman of the Building Committee, he still had to struggle to obtain a dissecting room and museum for his department.

Blackstone chair

BLOCK PLAN OF THE NEW BUILDINGS.

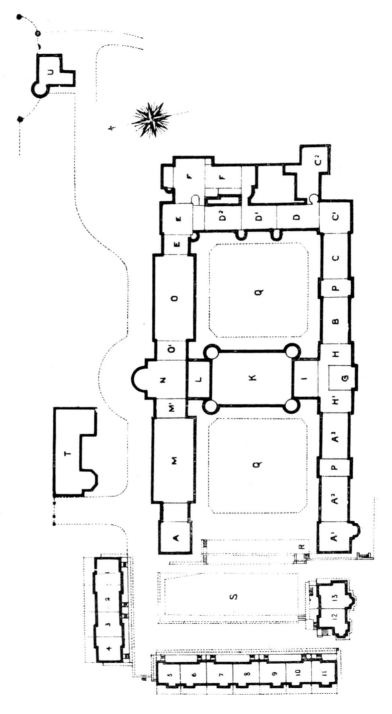

SCALE.

24

A. Greek, Logic, and Moral Philosophy Class Rooms in the three floors.

A¹. Latin, Mathematics, and Engineering and Mechanics.

A². English Literature and Astronomy (in Attics, Engineering and Mechanics Work Rooms).

A³. Physical Laboratory, (and above the Archway P.) Natural Philosophy Class Room and Apparatus Room.

B. Law Class Rooms and Examination Hall (also above P.).

C. Hebrew, Church History, and Biblical Criticism Class Rooms (in Attics, Divinity Hall Library), and in part Chemistry.

C¹. Chemistry Class Rooms, Divinity Hall.

C². Chemistry Laboratories (and in part below D.).

D. Medical Jurisprudence Class Room and Laboratory, Midwifery Class Room, &c.

D¹. Physiology Laboratories and Class Room, Practice of Physic Class Room.

D². Botanical Laboratory, Materia Medica Class Room. In Attics over D, D¹. and D²., Natural History Store Rooms, &c.

EE. Natural History, Surgery, and Hunterian Anatomy Collections.

FF. Anatomy Class Room and Laboratories, &c., extending also below D². and E.

G. Tower, Principal Entrance, Clerk of Senate's Office, &c.

H. Staircase and Corridor.

H¹. Senate Room and Corridor.

I. Matriculation Office, Cloak Room, Randolph Hall.

K. Cloisters and Bute Hall.

L. University Court Room, Antiquities Room, Hunterian Coins Room, Randolph Staircase.

M. Library Halls, Upper and Lower.

M¹. Library Service Room and Ante-rooms.

N. Students' Reading Room below, Central Hall of Hunterian Museum above.

O. Hunterian Museum Halls, Upper and Lower.

O¹. Ante-rooms, &c., of Museum.

PP. Entrances to East and West Quadrangles (QQ).

R. Old College Stair.

S. Professors' Court and Residences of Principal and Professors (1 to 13).

T. Students' Union.

U. North East Lodge, Naval Architecture Class Rooms.

Block plan of the new buildings on Gilmorehill

William Tennant Gairdner

THE medical school was, indeed, placed in some risk by the move to Gilmorehill. Students found themselves at a distance of three miles from their training ground in the Royal Infirmary. It had been originally intended that as well as a new University building a new University hospital should be built and when it became plain that sufficient funds would not be forthcoming, a separate appeal was launched on behalf of a Western Infirmary. By the autumn of 1870, however, the new hospital was far from complete and, from 1870 to 1874, students were conveyed daily "by a service of swift omnibuses" from the Royal Infirmary to their classes on Gilmorehill. The medical school survived until the opening of the infirmary in November 1874.

The opening day itself was not auspicious. Sir William Gairdner, Professor of Medicine during this period, described it with feeling.

"By an almost inconceivable procrastination in some quarter or another," he raged, "not a single patient had been admitted to the wards on the very day when the college was to resume its educational work, when the medical students were flocking into their classrooms from all quarters, and when the makeshift arrangements with the Royal had become impossible owing to the final severance – under directions – of the medical and surgical officers representing the University from their posts in the Royal Infirmary and their formal election to corresponding offices in the Western Infirmary."

But patients were not hard to find. Within twenty-four hours the beds were filled and the future of the famous Glasgow medical school was assured. In acknowledging the necessity whereby clinical education for medical students would be provided within the Western Infirmary, the way was opened to the future addition of laboratories and teaching units appropriate to the subjects taught.

Lord Kelvin

PRACTICAL demonstrations were still, however, given in lecture rooms, as a former student of Lord Kelvin remembered in the *Glasgow University Magazine* in the nineties.

"I was interested to notice that the old experiment of firing the rifle in the Natural Philosophy class is still performed", he wrote. "When, many years ago I was a member of the class, a very ancient looking blunderbuss was the weapon employed, and the vividest recollection that I have of my Physics course is that of the amazement on the Professor's face as he rose to his feet and the smoke cleared away when he saw in front of him an empty array of wooden benches. Sir William had not then made his reputation as a marksman and the class had to a man taken refuge beneath the desks."

THE two great political rivals, Gladstone and Disraeli, both served as rectors during the 1870's. Neither achieved this distinction at the first attempt but Disraeli was the first of the two to be installed at a ceremony in the Kibble Palace in the Botanic Gardens.

Not till nearly the end of the decade, in December 1879, did Gladstone follow him. He received a stormy reception from the students – again in the Kibble Palace. During the uproar, Sir John Mann recalled, "Gladstone rose and stood impassive, high above the tumult, awaiting the end of the din while professor upon professor vainly appealed with uplifted hands for silence.

"After a long time (one of my friends afterwards told me it was twenty minutes) the G.O.M. made up his mind that sufficient tribute had been paid to him. I recall vividly how he merely raised his hand and said 'Gentlemen'. Immediately all was still."

1880-1890

THE LAST LONG SUMMERS

AT the luncheon that followed Gladstone's installation as rector, reference was made to his sparing of valuable time to the "serene, if dull, seclusion of academic things". Gladstone quibbled at the word "dull". And certainly in the decade that followed in Glasgow, there was nothing dull about University affairs or those engaged in them.

WHILE the eighties saw far-reaching changes and innovations in the University, they were also the last years of the old régime with its concentration on traditional studies continued from the Old College. If, moreover, the middle of the eighteenth century is to be described as one Golden Age in the history of the University, then these two last decades of the nineteenth have a claim to be regarded as another.

In the Faculty of Arts, Jebb and then Gilbert Murray occupied the Chair of Greek, G. G. Ramsay that of Humanity, Edward Caird that of Moral Philosophy, A. C. Bradley that of English, and Phillimore presided first over the Greek and then – but in another century – over the Humanity classroom. The chair of Natural Philosophy was occupied by the man who has been described as "the greatest, most beloved, and most modest of them all, Lord Kelvin".

Medicine was dominated by Sir William Gairdner who created a "school" of Medicine as, later, Macewen did of Surgery and Muir of Pathology. Sir Robert Muir's predecessor in the Chair of Pathology was, moreover, Joseph Coats of whom a student commented that after working under him: "Immediately I became interested in Medicine; until then, I had simply accepted the fact that I was to be a doctor."

Richard Claverhouse Jebb   *Gilbert Murray*

"MOST attractive was the life of Professors in the Arts Faculty in those days", Professor J. M. Munro Kerr remembered. "The sessions of 22–24 weeks ended in April when down were pulled the blinds and up went brown paper in the windows of their houses and off they departed to their summer quarters – Ramsay to Drummore, his property in Perthshire; Veitch (of Logic) to Peebles beside his beloved Tweed; Lord Kelvin to his home on the shores of the Clyde, if experiments being carried out in his laboratory permitted. And not until October did they return to their official residences in the University. . . .

"It was largely because of those long vacations with opportunities for quiet study that the chairs in Scottish Universities were eagerly sought after by scholars like Jebb, Gilbert Murray, Phillimore, and Raleigh. Admittedly, the stay of some in Glasgow was of short duration but we had Jebb with us for 14 years, Gilbert Murray for 10 years, and Phillimore for life."

THIS long vacation came to an end in the eighties. The summer session was introduced by the Universities (Scotland) Act of 1889.

GILBERT MURRAY, who was only 23 when he was appointed to the Chair of Greek in 1889, wrote later of the strangeness – to him – of Glasgow at that period.

30

"I was very young when I was appointed Professor at Glasgow, I think only half the age of the youngest of my colleagues. I had not thought of standing for the chair but I was encouraged and, indeed, invited to apply. So I collected testimonials, bought a new top hat, and called on the Electors. . . .

"Many things were strange. It was rather strange having to collect one's salary in cash. One took three guineas from student by student for about three days, put the money each day into a stout leather bag and then, armed with a good stout walking stick, carried it to the Bank. I was once advised to have a companion with a real cudgel, but cannot remember whether I did so.

"I liked my students immensely. They were not as good at Greek as those I had had in Oxford but they were more fresh and more grateful for any trouble one took with them. . . . In Glasgow the most important element in an undergraduate's course was the Professor's lecture. Consequently the lecturers had to be fairly good. A lecturer had at least to lecture effectively – audibly and intelligibly and, if possible, interestingly – if he did not, the audience was restless and would 'rough' on the floor. Professor Raleigh used to say that no one in Oxford knew

Professor Gilbert Murray delivering his inaugural lecture

Queen Margaret College students

how to lecture unless he had had some training in a Scottish or provincial university.

"The women's course at Queen Margaret (College) was just starting in my time. It was a new idea and was supposed to be a formidable problem but was really no problem at all. The women students were a select few, all with strong intellectual tastes, and generally more eager to learn than the average of the men's classes."

NOT all Murray's colleagues shared his favourable opinion of the students at Queen Margaret College. While the separate classes continued at the College, their teachers referred to them, on occasion, in deprecating or, perhaps, subtly disapproving terms. "This lecture, gentlemen," one lecturer explained to his audience on Gilmorehill, "was prepared for the weaker intellects of Queen Margaret College."

Women students had begun, however, to impinge on the life of the University before the 1880's. The first occupant of the Chair of English, Professor John Nichol, had, earlier, arranged classes in English literature for ladies as well as gentlemen. In 1877, the Association for the Higher Education of Women in Glasgow and the West of Scotland had been formed with Princess Louise, Marchioness of Lorne, as president. The objective was the establishment of a College of the University exclusively for women and it was encouraged by Principal John Caird who urged women to continue "knocking at the door of the University till you get the honours you deserve".

In 1878 bursaries were made available to women and rooms were engaged in the St Andrews Halls for tutorial classes. Correspondence classes were arranged to enable girls at a distance to prepare for University examinations. By 1882, there were 470 students on the roll, including students from overseas. In the following year the association was incorporated as a college named the Queen Margaret College after the saintly wife of Malcolm Canmore.

The College itself was established in Northpark House on the banks of the Kelvin close to the Botanic Gardens (now the headquarters of the B.B.C. in Glasgow). The house had been built a few years earlier to designs by J. T. Rochead for John Bell of Bell's Pottery whose fame resided in – apart from his pottery – his distaste for women.

Princess Louise was honorary president of the College and in August 1888 it was visited by Queen Victoria. The visit was interpreted as an indication of the Queen's approval of her daughter's college and, hopefully, of her approval of higher education for women.

Queen Margaret College

"Queen Victoria's historic visit was an anxious time for the Council of the College and the students assembled on the front steps," one account stated, "and the story has been handed down that the royal carriage coming along the narrow Hamilton Drive missed the gate into the College grounds and, to the Queen's annoyance, had to drive all round the block once more and try again. Then one of the out-riders fell and the carriage had a nasty jolt when, in making a sweeping turn in front of the door, a wheel knocked over one of the iron lions guarding the lawn." The mishaps would have made that misogynistic old man, John Bell, very happy.

The end of the decade saw the passing of the Universities (Scotland) Act which, among other measures, abolished the custom which Gilbert Murray found so strange whereby students paid their fees directly to the professor. The Act was preceded, inevitably and necessarily, by lengthy controversy – in one sense, a controversy continued for more than a century – of such emotive issues as qualifications for admission and standards of teaching.

Classes, it was claimed by critical reformers, were swollen by immature students whose fees were, however, necessary to the maintenance of the professors. Fifteen or sixteen was still a common age of entrance. A few undergraduates matriculated at fourteen and even this was less precocious than Lord Kelvin who went up when he was a little over ten and John Gibson Lockhart, Scott's son-in-law and biographer, who went up at eleven.

In 1880, John Bright, the Liberal statesman, was elected Rector. In March 1883 he was installed at a ceremony in the St Andrews Halls. He received a more subdued welcome than Mr Gladstone. "Stout, benignant, with abundant grey locks," his rectorial address was, to begin with, low-keyed.

"But as he proceeded, he became excited, and one gesture was too dramatic," one report ran. "His outflung hand came down so sharply

Installation as Rector of John Bright

35

on the mace that the heavy head was broken off and fell with a resounding crash among the reporters. The orator stopped abruptly; his hand was seen to be bleeding. One of my friends thrust his handkerchief to the Bedellus whispering, "It's quite clean," and so the bleeding hand was bound up. . . . Then the great orator, holding up his bandaged hand for silence, continued unperturbed, the mace, its severed head handed back by the reporters, resting before him."

The Union Bazaar

IN 1885, a student resolution was carried in favour of forming a Glasgow University Union. Principal Caird lent the proposal his support, recalling as he did so the friendlessness and isolation he had himself experienced as a student in the 1840's.

The students set about raising funds for a building. A gift of £51,000 from Dr John McIntyre "to provide a memorial for his wife" provided a generous foundation and a grand bazaar was planned for the December of 1889. The editorial staff of the *Glasgow University Magazine* entered with enthusiasm on the task of whipping up interest in the enterprise.

Apart from the plethora of hand-worked smoking caps – to be fashioned by the sisters of the students – which the magazine commended as suitable merchandise, "The latest notion for a novelty at the ensuing Union Bazaar," it reported, "is a switchback railway. It is to start from one of the upper windows of the Medical Quadrangle, sweep down to the middle of the quad, and rise through the window space of the Bute Hall, and will finish at the Professors' Houses. This proposal, we understand, originated with a professor."

The bazaar, and the torchlight procession which preceded it, was an outstanding success. The money needed was raised. Afterwards, the University, both staff and students, relaxed with a sense of achievement. For, *G.U.M.* elaborated, "not only has the Bazaar raised money for our Union but it has done yeoman service in the way of helping us carry out the objects for which the Union was founded. It has brought all ranks and classes of students together in the prosecution of a common object; it has connected together professors and students in ways that they never were connected before; it has brought recluses out of their dens and subjected them to the beguiling influences of female charms and it has revealed that there is a musical and dramatic talent in Glasgow University that was never previously suspected."

RELATIONS between students and professors were usually cordial and frequently informal. An exception was the November "capping" in 1889. It was to be held in the Randolph Hall and students, the word had gone round, were to be excluded because at recent ceremonies, they had been the source of considerable disorder.

The students decided that the ceremony should be allowed to go so far – then they would storm the Randolph Hall. Their attack broke up the end of the graduation ceremony and, in the scuffle that followed, the "Magister Cap" was captured. It was, however, an embarrassing acquisition and its captors didn't quite know what to do with or about it. They decided finally to return it to the Senate, with an admonitory note to the effect that the Senate should not repeat the mistake of that day.

IN 1889, the first issue of the *Glasgow University Magazine* appeared. The first number, price one penny, was published on February 5th. Within a short time, it was being celebrated in the following terms:

> "The *G.U.M.*, the *G.U.M.*!
> Where inky bards have often sung,
> Its scribes for nothing give a dem,
> The Editor is still unhung;
> And all good Christians will regret,
> The staff at large is roaming yet."

The opening of the Bute Hall

THE new buildings at Gilmorehill – completed with the addition of the spire and the Bute and Randolph Halls, designed by J. Oldrid Scott – took care of the "mens sana". The organisation of facilities for sport accompanied the building programme on the hill. The University "field" in the eighties was a piece of ground between the professors' houses and the Western Infirmary. There was a gymnasium and by the end of 1884, tennis courts and a running track.

Cycle racing on the old high bicycle was the paramount attraction at sports meetings at this period and Glasgow University Athletic Club's cinder track placed it "in a favourable position for catering for this popular and exciting sport".

A WIDELY appreciated addition to the plenishings of the University about which, however, comparatively little is known, was made during the 1880's. These were the University bells which were cast in 1888 by the firm of Taylor of Loughborough. The two small bells form the chime and the large bell – weighing 57 cwt 3 qr 1 lb – strikes the hour.

The chapel bell, seventeenth-century in date, spent several decades in exile in the Blackfriars Kirk in Dennistoun after the move to Gilmorehill: on the completion of the new University Chapel it regained its ancient function.

The University Bells

The hurry bell

The chapel bell

1890-1900

WHO "LECTURE SO AWFULLY WELL"

"WITH all that books can give us, there is still an invaluable element of education which can reach us only through living contact with the mind and personality of a teacher who is master of his subject." Thus Principal John Caird in April 1894.

HE had still four years to go as principal, an office in which he enjoyed the admiration of his students to a remarkable degree. Widely regarded as the finest preacher of his time, none who heard him, it was claimed, "could forget his leonine features and long, iron-grey locks; and his rich resonant voice with a curious and effective break which he introduced into it to emphasise his argument when roused to a high pitch of oratory."

Students deprived of the opportunity to hear him preach complained to, among others, the editor of *G.U.M.* of the unsatisfactory arrangements made.

"SIR, – You are probably aware that the Principal generally preaches to the students and the public at large four times at most in the session. The majority, however, of the Arts students have not the privilege of sitting under him on all these occasions. Somehow or other, the Sunday fixed for the Principal's sermon in February has, for the last three years, preceded the Candlemas holidays. Now, as the holidays occur on a Monday and Tuesday, the general body of the Arts men invariably go home on the Friday before, and consequently lose their chance of hearing the Principal. The students can ill afford to miss an opportunity of hearing the Principal and one and all would like if those, whose duty

Principal John Caird preaching

it is to fix the preachers for the University Chapel, would kindly change the date in February and save a great amount of grumbling."

In Logic and Moral Philosophy, Edward Caird – Principal Caird's brother – and John Veitch made of Glasgow "a veritable nursery of budding Professors of Philosophy". Caird's translation to the mastership of Balliol in 1894 grieved his students. "Oh Oxonia!" they lamented, not without an eye to the effect created, "We are bereaved indeed!" He was succeeded in the Moral Philosophy classroom by Henry Jones, splendidly described by Thomas Jones as "wrapping his toga round him as he trod his rostrum, like an admiral his quarter-deck, overwhelming us all with the Celtic fervour of his oratory, assuming the appearance of a major prophet as he rose to the grand climax of a lecture with Kant's ringing affirmation of faith: 'Two things fill me with awe and wonder – the starry heavens above and the moral law within'."

In the Humanity classroom, Professor George Gilbert Ramsay bore down heavily on the slipshod and unprepared among his students. "Why are you unprepared Jacobus Johnston?" he shouted at one student who happened to be older than the others. The wretched man stammered: "My wife had a baby this morning". Ramsay didn't hear him correctly and replied: "Don't let it happen again".

In Mathematics, Professor William Jack led his students tranquilly through the mazes of mathematics. "Produce the line from AB to L", a student suggested when faced with a geometrical problem. "Better keep it within the University grounds", the professor advised.

THE stay in Glasgow of Professor Richard Lodge of the Chair of History was comparatively short but it was long enough for him to impress his personality on his students.

> "There was a Professor R.L.
> Who never would stop for the bell,
> When his class showed their ire
> He said: How can you tire
> When I lecture so awfully well?"

Lodge was a Liberal and he was appalled by Joseph Chamberlain's rectorial address on "Patriotism". On the day after Chamberlain's installation, he devoted his lecture to correction of its distortions. "It is not my business to discuss the politics of the Lord Rector", he informed his class, "but it is my duty to see that you get your history right."

The Chair of English was occupied at this period by A. C. Bradley who, like some other incomers from the south, seems to have found the Glasgow climate trying. On one occasion he burst into rhyming complaint of his lack of avoirdupois with which to combat it.

> "Were I but fat I should not freeze,
> This sooty snow might do its worst;
> The North might bellow till he burst
> If only I were more obese."

Edward Caird

G. G. Ramsay

William Jack

A. C. Bradley

He was succeeded by Walter Raleigh who had some years before followed him at Liverpool. "I regard him," Raleigh said of Bradley in his inaugural lecture, "as one appointed by Providence to make my way in life difficult for me. I am afraid that this is not a business of which the good-will can be handed over in a day." When Raleigh left Glasgow, however, it was to occupy the newly established chair of English at Oxford or, as he himself said when asked what he would do at Oxford: "Tosh and Text – and I shall do the Tosh".

But probably the most famous lecture anecdote concerns Lord Kelvin though it does not, strictly, belong to this decade. His lectures were, apparently, less than lucid but he had an assistant called Day whose expositions of the mysteries of Natural Philosophy were. When Professor William Thomson, as he was at the time, was summoned to London to receive the accolade of knighthood, he returned to find inscribed on the blackboard of his classroom: "Work while ye have yet Day for the Knight cometh when no man can work".

In 1896, his jubilee in the Chair of Natural Philosophy was celebrated. Guests at the celebrations were requested "on leaving to pass out by the staircase at the Museum. . . ."

These last years of the nineteenth century were vintage years among the students. The most widely known of them in later life was, probably, John Buchan, later Lord Tweedsmuir, Governor-General of Canada, but better known as the author of *The Thirty-Nine Steps, Huntingtower,* and *Montrose.*

"In my day, a Scottish University still smacked of the Middle Ages", he wrote in his autobiography. "The undergraduates lived in lodgings in the city and most of them cultivated the Muses on a slender allowance of oatmeal. The session ran from October to April and every morning I had to walk four miles to the eight o'clock class through every variety of the winter weather with which Glasgow fortifies her children. . . .

"As a student I was wholly obscure. I made few friends; I attended infrequently one or other of the numerous societies, but I never spoke in a debate; and I acquired the corporate spirit only at a rectorial election, when, as a professed Tory, I chose to support the Liberal candidate, Mr Asquith, and almost came by my end at the hands of a red-haired savage, one Robert Horne, who has since been Chancellor of the Exchequer".

Rectorial election of A. J. Balfour

THE red-haired savage, Robert S. Horne – later Viscount Horne – played a prominent part in student life of the period as president of the S.R.C. as well as of the Conservative Club. He also played a prominent part in the riot at the Ice Skating Palace in Sauchiehall Street (on the site of what later, at various periods, became Hengler's Circus and the Regal Cinema). The affair followed the torchlight procession that formed part of the election as rector of Joseph Chamberlain in 1896.

At the private view of the "Real Ice Palace," Sauchiehall Street

When the procession was over, its participants felt the night was too young for them to go home, and they adjourned to the Skating Palace. The management was not, however, disposed to admit them and having failed to persuade them to go away, turned fire hoses on them. The students besieged the building and all the windows on the front of it were broken. Some of the leaders of the student societies attempted to restore order. But the police, under the impression that they were inciting their followers to further outrages, arrested them. Horne survived the fracas to become Conservative M.P. for Hillhead, Minister of Labour, President of the Board of Trade, and Chancellor of the Exchequer.

At Hengler's Cirque

The same decade produced Lord MacMillan of Aberfeldy whose career as a barrister in England as well as Scotland was distinguished, and who delivered in June 1951 the commemorative address of the Fifth Centenary celebrations: Lord Lindsay of Birker, Master of Balliol, Thomas Jones, Deputy Secretary of the Cabinet: and Dame Louise McIlroy, one of the pioneers of women in Medicine. It produced too two authors whose best-known works could scarcely have been more different – J. J. Bell, the creator of "Wee MacGreegor", the epitome of small, taiblet-devouring Glasgow boys, and George Douglas Brown, Snell Exhibitioner in 1891, and author of *The House with the Green Shutters*.

STUDENTS of the 1890's were much exercised about lecturing standards – "Wanted, very badly, a lectureship on public reading and speaking", *G.U.M.* claimed – and the question of academic dress. On the first question, printed lectures were suggested.

"There is a movement in College just now by which it is proposed to do away with notebooks altogether at lectures. A number of students are combining to employ a shorthand writer in each class where lectures are given. The shorthand notes will then be sent straight to the printer and the requisite number of copies be sent to the subscribers on the following day."

The title of the proposed company was to be "The Society for the Abolition of Anachronistic Methods in University Teaching".

As regards academic dress, controversy raged as to whether students should wear gowns and trenchers, caps, or no academic dress at all. The principal argument of the advocates of some form of dress was that it would make students "quite distinct from ordinary people who make rows at places of amusement". Their opponents claimed that it was "a little disgusting to think of a man going about in a gown which has served the purpose of keeping his clothes clean in the dissecting room".

There were those who suggested distinguishing caps. One correspondent of *G.U.M.* inclined to a velvet cap such as that worn by students in Paris "rather loose and flat, adorned by a broad silk ribbon – each faculty possessing a different colour. It curls", the writer added persuasively, "very gracefully over one's ear."

Medical students, it was suggested, should wear a black velvet cap with a gold tassel. "Ever so many ideas have been put forward for a distinguishing costume," *G.U.M.* eventually declared wearily, "even to the picturesque idea of chimney pot and kilt."

A plebiscite was taken and it was discovered that of the 501 votes cast, 334 were for gown and trencher, 99 for no academic dress, and 68 for a cap. Just over half the votes cast came from Arts students.

DISTINGUISHING dress was, however, hardly necessary when the Glasgow students elected to spend a night at the theatre, usually the

Academic Dress

As it too often appears

As it should be

Students entertained

Students entertaining

Royalty in Sauchiehall Street. Though many of them were connoisseurs of the light opera, their object in going to the theatre was as much to entertain as to be entertained.

They occupied the "gods" and once settled in their places, began the programme of student songs with which they enlivened the beginning, intervals and conclusion of the official entertainment. The *G.U.M.* critic, reviewing their performance, called on one occasion for a little more nerve and vigour. He turned, too, a disapproving eye on those students who failed to behave in a gentlemanly manner. "Those adherents of the Son of Belial," he commented acidly, "who persisted at the back in sampling from lemonade bottles what was evidently the choicest blend of the Chronic Club's usquebaugh, might please do it less openly next time."

AT Queen Margaret College, the objective of equality of educational opportunity was brought gradually closer by the energy and tact of Janet Galloway who served first as voluntary secretary of the Glasgow Association for the Higher Education of Women, then as secretary of Queen Margaret College, and later of the Women's Department of the University.

The kind of prejudice she encountered is summed up in one student's dismissal of women students: "Women students are so called by courtesy; it is well known that they can be sharply differentiated into classes – those who are students and those who are women. I have not yet heard of any unclassified exception who might be described as both."

The proposal of a Medical School for Women won her enthusiastic support. With the help of Professor John Young (of Natural History), Mrs Campbell of Tullichewan, and Mrs John Elder (to whom Queen Margaret College owed the roof over their heads) she carried it through and in 1894, Marion Gilchrist graduated in medicine, the first woman to do so at a Scottish university. The window in the Bute Hall which the colleagues and friends of Janet

Janet Galloway

Galloway presented to the University in her memory represents appropriately the pursuit of ideal education and its results, service, fame, devotion, and spiritual vision.

In the 1880's and 1890's, the idea of service took on particular meaning in Glasgow as the appalling poverty, ill-health, and squalor endured by a large proportion of the city's inhabitants were exposed by, notably, the public speeches of the Medical Officer of Health, Dr James Burn Russell. A succession of Acts of Parliament cleared the way to the demolition of some of the more pestiferous slums and the introduction of provisions for the improvement of the city's health. A number of universities established settlements in slum areas during this period and their action reflected their wish both to know the size of the social problem of their doorstep and to do something about it.

William Smart, lecturer in Political Economy in Queen Margaret College, visited in 1886 the recently established Toynbee Hall in the East End of London. In November of the same year, the Glasgow University Settlement Association was established which took part of a house in Townhead and named it Toynbee House. There, social and educational good works were carried out in one of the worst slum areas in the city.

In 1889, the Students Settlement in Possil Road was founded by a group of Divinity students guided by Professor Henry Drummond of the Free Church College: gradually its importance in the life of Glasgow surpassed that of Toynbee House.

Thomas Jones, later Deputy Secretary to the Cabinet, remembered the rigours of work there. "The neighbourhood was poor and overcrowded and one would need the hide of a rhinoceros to be indifferent to the misery around us or to be satisfied with prescribing Moody and Sankey's evangelical salvation as the one and only remedy. I was allotted a close which had 44 families in 44 rooms on six floors off one staircase. . . . We went about, as it was said, unpacking our hopes of a blissful future with a New Testament in one pocket and a Fabian tract in the other, seeking to reconcile the otherworldliness of the one and the this-worldliness of the other."

1900-1910

ON A DAILY ALLOWANCE OF TWO SHILLINGS

THE University entered on the twentieth century with a celebration of its ninth jubilee. The events of June 13th 1901 were, it was later reported by one participant, "a reasonable day's programme" – two orations (by Lord Kelvin and Professor William Smart); a conferring of honorary degrees in which one of the graduands was Mr Andrew Carnegie; luncheon; the opening of the new Botanical Building; a garden party at Queen Margaret College; a dinner party and – the official account of the celebrations stated – "the entertainments of a well-filled day were wound up by a great Conversazione".

Pearce Lodge: drawing by Muirhead Bone

"At the beginning of the new century her hopes are bright," J. H. Muir (the pen name under which Muirhead Bone, James Bone, and A. H. Charteris wrote *Glasgow in 1901*) wrote of the University. "Her students number nearly 1700 men and 350 women. She has thirty-two professors and forty-one assistants and if the West of Scotland maintains its traditional name for generosity, her credit-balance which in 1899–1900 was £138, will be changed into something less depressing".

From the crest of Gilmorehill in that year of 1901, the University looked down on some remarkable sights for it was the year of the second of the Glasgow Exhibitions (the first was held in 1888). The pavilions were set up on the opposite bank of the Kelvin. The general theme was the development of industry, art and science, lightened, however, by – among other attractions – gondolas on the Kelvin propelled by two genuine Venetian gondoliers known locally as Signor Hokey and Signor Pokey, and the music of John Philip Sousa conducted by the composer.

For both professors and students, life was still spacious and leisurely on Gilmorehill. "On a daily allowance of two shillings a man could pay his tram fares, pay for his tobacco and his lunch and have something left over for coffee. He might be ploughed a dozen times only to come up smiling for the thirteenth round," L. J. Russell, a student at this period who later occupied the Chair of Philosophy at Birmingham, remembered.

"I couldn't afford to join the Union," he added, "which cost 7s 6d a year or to have coffee, but there were free periods in which one met people and walked and talked. . . . It was possible, if not easy, to keep finances straight. Fees were paid by the Carnegie Trust and I had an open bursary of £30 a year for four years but this, after providing the necessary text books, was needed at home. Ten shillings a month pocket money had to cover fares and subscriptions and all odd expenses, including ties, handkerchiefs, and gloves."

J. H. Muir's account – slightly earlier for the Union subscription is still five shillings – is more sombre.

"His (the student's) life is plain and hard and rather poor in colour. His class at eight a.m. calls him early from his bed – and how early he who comes to it by train from the suburbs will tell you. And what, after all, comes he out for to see? The tardy moon lighting him up the College hill, the windy quadrangle all dark, the lighted classroom

Humanity Classroom

windows, a brisk janitor selling the College magazine, the College bell, clattering for five short minutes after the hour has struck, its sudden stop, the scramble of men to enter while yet there is time, the roll-call, the lecture, the bent heads of the note-takers, the scraping of their anxious feet lest a word be missed, the rustling of a sporting paper, the smell of wet waterproof in the hot air, the intolerable dreichness of (let us say) the Conveyancing Statutes, and then – happy release! – the College clock booming out the hour and once more the rain and the wind in the quadrangle. No handsome reward this for early rising!"

BUT there were rewards. There were, for example, John Swinnerton Phillimore's lectures in the Greek classroom and, after 1906, in the Humanity classroom. The Greek class met at eight and Phillimore breakfasted after he had lectured and not before. "He usually wore a suit of rough tweed and in appearance he was less formally academic than some of his colleagues. . . . His good humour was imperturbable and I cannot remember that even the slightest disturbance occurred in his classes," Professor Russell wrote. "He had completely adopted the Scottish way of pronouncing Greek though he must for years have been accustomed to the English practice."

55

His choice of material for prose composition was unconventional. "Chesterton appeared more than once in passages from his essays; Hazlitt; Newman from *Callista*; and (in 1904) part of the Mikado's declaration of war against Russia." In 1906, he moved to Humanity where he was "a Latinist who could make Latinists, whose scholarship had a sweep that embraced all Latinity and a subtlety that first amazed and then delighted".

He was, too, a notable contributor to *G.U.M.* "Which editor thought of bringing out his Christmas Number without the ballade signed J.S.P. ?," the magazine mourned when he died.

D. J. Medley

A few doors away, Lodge's successor, Professor Dudley Medley – Deadly Muddly an irreverent student nick-named him – presided over the History classroom. He began his career clean-shaven but in the autumn of 1910, it was alleged, on the platform at Crewe, he decided to grow a beard. One result of the change was to enhance his resemblance to King Charles I. Medley himself was well aware of the resemblance and secretly rather proud of it, "though it did not", one of his students solemnly averred, "in any way affect his course of lectures on the early Stuarts".

His interests were not, however, confined to the teaching of history. He was a member of the Glasgow School Board and added his support to the newly established Glasgow and West of Scotland Commercial College. On Gilmorehill itself, worried by the absence of communication between the University and its students and graduates, he was instrumental in the development of the Officers' Training Corps, and in the institution of the annual conversaziones for graduates.

Though the conversaziones were a success, it took some time before the suspicions of graduates were dispelled. One, on receiving his invitation to meet members of the Court and Senate, accompanied his refusal with the observation that he had no wish to meet these gentlemen in this world and no fear of meeting them in the next.

ANOTHER of Professor Medley's interests was the Appointments Committee of which he was the second chairman (the first was Professor Robert Latta of Logic). The Committee was established by the Senate in January 1903 "for the purpose of collecting and communicating information regarding appointments suitable for students and graduates". It existed for 27 months when no more than 25 graduates registered whose ages suggested that "a considerable number of the applicants are in the stickit class". There already existed the Committee on Civil Service and External Examinations and it was from this that, after 1911, the present Appointments Committee developed.

IN 1907 an important break with tradition took place in the University. Robert Herbert Story, who had succeeded Caird as Principal, died. His successor, Donald MacAlister, was Glasgow's first lay Principal. Sir Donald (in the year after his appointment he was created K.C.B.), who had qualified in Medicine and was president of the General Medical Council, was excellently equipped to watch over Glasgow's fast-growing Medical School and during this period, the connection with the Royal Infirmary, interrupted by the move to Gilmorehill, was restored.

THE Glasgow Medical School also acquired in 1905 two distinguished medical students though their distinctions were rather extra-curricular than otherwise. They were O. H. Mavor (James Bridie) and Walter Elliot under whose direction G.U.M. (of which they were successively editors) flourished as it had never done before. Most of their poems and the drawings signed OH! are still entombed in the back numbers of G.U.M. but in 1910 a selection of verses that had appeared in G.U.M. between 1903 and 1910 was published. The illustrations were, of course, by OH! The introduction was supplied by Professor Phillimore who described himself as the

> "Superfluous showman of the favourite Troop,
> Bowing as low as middle age can stoop."

Elliot, writing as "Parvus" devoted himself, for the most part, to praise of the pleasures of eating. Mavor, signing himself – in this volume – The Squid, contributed, among other verses, the wry lyric that begins:

> "Bring me rich jewels for my love and damasks rich and rare,
> And nard and spice of Orient and ouches for her hair,
> And bring her silks and bring her lace and charge them up to me,
> For ah! My love is forty five and I am twenty three."

II.—THE ARRIVAL

THERE was Academic Arty and Lawd Chawlie in a suit
  That petrified the porter on the pier;
And Arty brought the baggage, and Lawd Chawlie
  brought his flute,
  And the Present Scribe was bringing up—the rear.

J.S.P. is included too, notably in his translation of the Emperor Hadrian's "Animula, blandula, vagula. . . ."

"Little slip of a soul, my pretty sweeting,
  Whither away truant, whither afresh,
  To what new world wilt thou be fleeting,
  Lodger and playmate of the flesh?
  – Wan, chilly, naked and diminished,
  And all the old fun finished."

O. H. Mavor (James Bridie)

Walter Elliot

WALTER ELLIOT was president of the Union and entertained his friends generously at his flat. Later, he entered Parliament and became Minister of Agriculture and Secretary of State for Scotland. In 1957 the students of his University elected him their rector.

During an election campaign in Kelvingrove which he represented for many years in Parliament, he received a note from a constituent:

"Dear Sir,
For years you and your student friends kept me awake till all hours

Another Union, but the same fire

of the morning. To show that I bear you no malice, I propose to vote for you at this election."

The Great Chronics flourished at this period. The Greatest of them gathered, Walter Elliot wrote, in the Warblers' Room in the Union. How great they were may be realised from this that James Bridie did not even begin to qualify as one of their number. Lesser chronics, and others, gathered in the Secretary's Room where "you could get coffee for a penny and a beautiful pink iced cake for the same sum; and all morning successive waves of men used to come and go, join in the songs, stoke the fire, pay for round after round of coffee and cakes, and harangue, till newcomers had to fight their way in and make room for themselves by cutting out a chunk of air and throwing it from the window."

"The mere existence of famous teachers about the place was a liberal education whether one went near them or not," Elliot wrote. "At any moment, one might decide to do so . . . there were classes which one always hoped to get round to. There was Geology, for instance, under Gregory who had scaled Kilimanjaro, sleeping out at nights, when Kilimanjaro was not so very easy to find, let alone to climb. There was John Graham Kerr, of Zoology, who had theories of education drawn from years of residence among his friends, the South American aborigines, in search of lepidosirens."

In November 1909, Mavor was one of the spectators in the Coliseum Music Hall when Glasgow's medical students exacted their revenge on

TO MURPHY BODIE—IN ALL LOVE AND CHARITY—
HIS PICTURE.

*The Merry Devil –
"Dr" Walford Bodie*

the self-styled Dr Walford Bodie. "The Famous Bloodless Surgeon" was performing there for a week with his "Cage of Death" and had seen fit to deliver a speech to the audience on the opening night on the subject of medical students in general and the "Carnegie Cads" on Gilmorehill in particular. On the Thursday evening, the students descended on the music hall, their pockets bulging with ammunition (peasemeal, ochre, eggs ancient and modern, etc.).

The turns preceding Bodie's were galloped through at top speed. The 'doctor's' appearance was greeted by a hail of missiles from which he immediately fled. The stage manager lowered the safety curtain but the audience invaded the stage to find behind the curtain an array of policemen with, according to Mavor, "batons drawn and battle in their eyes." Collaboration between a police lieutenant and an ex-president of the Union, C. P. Williamson, restored an approximation of order and Williamson led the terror-stricken Bodie on stage to apologise to the students.

It was not quite the end of the evening. Having defended medicine from the incursions of quacks such as Bodie, the students decided to issue a like warning to two other quacks who lived in the city. The police, however, having wind of their intention, intervened and prevented the demonstrations.

At Queen Margaret College, the students were turning their minds to, arguably, higher things. The Queen Margaret College Suffrage Society was formed and it was addressed by Miss Christabel Pankhurst. "Taking it for granted that every one present was in favour of the principle of Woman Suffrage," G.U.M. reported, "Miss Pankhurst proceeded to explain why women had abandoned ladylike methods of agitation and had taken to their present unconstitutional methods of propaganda. . . . The meeting closed with three cheers for Miss Pankhurst and the singing of 'For She's a Jolly Good Fellow'."

During this decade too, Queen Margaret students widened their interest in and experience of Glasgow's social problems. In 1901, the Queen Margaret Settlement was opened in Anderston, described in the first report as "a very populous and very poor quarter of the city". Seven years later, it moved to Port Street, Anderston and the executive council announced that it would be glad "to receive applications from ladies who wish to enter the Settlement as residents. The terms for board are 21s weekly".

From the Settlement, a Collecting Savings Bank was organised with the aim of inculcating thrift among its neighbours. "The eagerness with which the women await the arrival of the collector with their card and money ready," the Settlement report stated, "shows that they appreciate the trouble taken to assist them in cultivating habits of thrift."

Collectors were welcomed, by swarms of children shouting: "Maw, the bank lady!"

A school for invalid and defective children, a milk depot, an "infant health visitation scheme", a clinic for mothers, these were some of the settlement's enterprises. In 1909, the first lecture on "Social Economics" was given with a view to the development of a School of Social Science and thus began the long association between the Settlement and the School of Social Study.

1910-1920

AN INTERESTING SPECTACLE

"But stay! The Muse has brought
O such a funny thought.
Imagine it, our gallant little band,
The staunch and ever ready O.T.C.,
Fighting and falling for its native land,
An interesting spectacle it would be."

The signature in *G.U.M.* is "Aramis"; the verse appeared in the O.T.C. number of the 1911–12 session. Aramis was Arthur Lang who was himself killed on the Somme in 1916.

ALTHOUGH the First World War and its aftermath dominated, obviously, recollections of this decade, the years before 1914 were far from uneventful. The events were of a less serious nature, admittedly, though this was not how they seemed at the time.

The decade began, as the previous one had done, with another Glasgow Exhibition, this time a piece of private enterprise (its predecessors had been backed by Glasgow Corporation) directed at raising sufficient funds to endow a Chair of Scottish History and Literature at the University of Glasgow.

The scheme provoked violent controversy for two reasons. There were those who questioned the need for such a chair. And there were others who questioned the method chosen for raising the necessary funds.

During the preliminaries to the exhibition, Professor Dudley Medley opposed the establishment of the chair on the grounds that he himself

1911 Exhibition –
Palace of Industries

made adequate provision for instruction in Scottish History. He deplored the agitation for the chair and claimed that its establishment could only encourage regrettable nationalist sentiments. A letter to the editor of the *Glasgow Herald* suggested that "the best thing Mr Medley can do when the Chair of Scottish History is founded, is to enrol himself as one of the first students." The exhibition went forward and Professor Medley grew a beard.

THE most vigorous criticism of the method chosen to raise the £15,000 needed came from David Murray, a member of the University Court and, later, the author of the lovingly compiled *Memories of the Old College of Glasgow*. The exhibition was to be an historical one and they would, he claimed, never make any money out of it. "Everybody knew that the money would be raised by the sideshows . . . they had simply put the University on the same footing as one of these sideshows – such as water-chutes, flip-flap, cinematograph and the skittle alley, the tea-room, the drinking bar, the smoking parlour, and the other adjuncts of a variety entertainment."

The exhibition as it was finally constituted must have pleased him not at all. It contained, certainly, replicas of an old Scottish burgh and a Highland clachan. The relevance of the Laplander and West African settlements that turned up in it must, however, have been difficult to explain. Visitors to the exhibition were addicted to singing "Abide with me". The melancholy strains of "Change and decay in all around I see", floated up to Gilmorehill.

But in April 1912, the University Court was informed that suffi-cient funds were available to allow an appointment to be made to the new chair. Robert S. Rait, later the Principal of the University, was appointed.

GLASGOW students too were addicted to singing. Some of their professors tolerated their concerts, some disliked them. Professor Medley insisted that "at the very least the musical efforts of his class should cease when he entered the room". The *pièce de resistance* of Phillimore's Humanity Class was, by one account, "Ye Mariners of England".

"It was the custom then to have a song and chorus as the students assembled in the class-rooms, and if a member of a class was reputed to be a good singer," Mr Finlayson, Bedellus from 1903–23, recalled, "he was asked to sing, and if he did not respond the next one heard was 'Pass him up'. He was immediately collared and passed up over the students' heads till he was dropped at the back of the classroom. Woe betide him if he wriggled on the way up. If he had sense he would go up like a board."

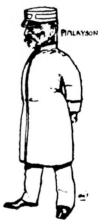

The Bedellus,
Mr Finlayson

THE University's O.T.C. prospered exceedingly during this period. Twenty cadets attended the coronation of King George V in June 1911. A recruiting poster supplied instructions as to how to join and

How to Join the Corps.

Go to Headquarters and get an Enrolment Form from the Sergeant-Major. Fill it up and return it with Ten Shillings Enrolment Fee.

CONDITIONS of ENLISTMENT.

15 Parades per Year (30 if a Recruit).

Attendance at Camp.

Musketry Course (Infantry and Engineers).

ADJUTANT.

Captain GRANT TAYLOR, R.S.F.

STAFF.

R.S.M. KERR, R.E.

Sergt. LAST, R.B.

Sergt. DUGMORE, R.A.M.C.

ADVANTAGES.

IF NECESSARY IT WILL MAKE A MAN OF YOU.

BADMINTON AND BOXING AT H.Q.

COURSES AT CHATHAM AND ALDERSHOT.

ATHLETICS.

O.T.C. Advertisement   **God Save the King.**

information on the advantages of doing so: "If necessary," it claimed, "it will make a man of you."

Graham Andrew wrote, "Like many others, I fell a victim to the siren voice of Cameron of Lochiel and joined that famous 'B' Company of the 6th Cameron Highlanders who, clad in most unmilitary garments, marched down Sauchiehall Street midst the plaudits of the good citizens of Glasgow."

"A year later on the bloody field of Loos . . . only a remnant of that gallant company answered the roll-call at the end of a battle which had taken as heavy a toll of the flower of our Scottish youth as our country had paid since the days of Flodden; but they had written one of the most glorious pages in the annals of the University of Glasgow."

THE survivors brought back accounts of unexpected meetings. One was reported in *G.U.M.* in 1918. "The scene was the Menin Road . . . the time a sultry day in July of last year. A battalion was passing through the ruins of a village, a Scottish regiment to judge from the cut of the officers' tunics, for the battalion was going into action and identification marks were absent; the men were more travel stained than usual, their faces streaked with sweat and dust.

"From the rear of the marching column the sound of a song with a not unfamiliar ring came down the breeze. But before one could recognise the air or the words the half dozen gallant singers in the column had come abreast and the words rang out clearly –

"Corabella, Corabella; Ching, Ching, Chingo!"

". . . The battalion, one learned later, belonged to a division which on Gallipoli had earned for itself the title of "Incomparable", and surely it was fitting that they, if any, should be called upon to join in singing an incomparable song."

BACK on Gilmorehill, meanwhile, work continued though under difficulties. The outbreak of war had found the Principal and Lady MacAlister in Germany from which they won their way home, however, without undue hardship. Many if not most professors dispensed with the increasingly depressing formality of rollcall: an exception was the Humanity Class where bench censors checked attendances.

The External Examiner.
(From the Verdun poster.)

THE war ended but there remained for the University one piece of unfinished business. Early in the war, the students had elected as their Rector Raymond Poincaré, President of the French Republic, and he had still to be installed. As the date of installation approached, the authorities – the Entente Cordiale and Auld Alliance notwithstanding – were apprehensive of his reception and his reaction. Attendance at the ceremony in the St Andrews Halls was, accordingly, limited. The lunch after the installation was to take place in the Bute Hall and eventually distinguished visitors began to arrive for it from the St Andrews Halls. "One of them, a haughty military gentleman, asked my group patronisingly", one student reported, "how to get to the dining hall. Sir Donald (MacAlister) happened to come up the stairs while we were conducting him there. Taking in the situation Sir Donald began to lay about him with his cane. It seemed he was being ushered to the ladies' cloakroom."

M. Poincaré did not greatly enjoy his visit. A snowstorm delayed his train and he reached Glasgow to find it shrouded in fog. His audience behaved decorously but when he arrived at the University, he was carried shoulder-high from the cloisters to the Bute Hall. On his return to France, he ungratefully described Scottish students as the most brutal in Europe.

Visit of President Poincaré for Rectorial Installation

"THE war to end war is at an end," *G.U.M.* pronounced, "and the future lies still in the lap of the gods."

Reactions of returning ex-servicemen to study and the University varied. There were those whose ambition it was "to enjoy untrammelled the sweets of a carefree University existence before the shades of the prison-house finally closed upon me. It was pleasant to wander about the old familiar quads, the cynosure of all eyes (or so one fondly supposed) in a trim officer's uniform complete with medal ribbons and gold wound stripes. This, I may say," Graham Andrew added, "was not youthful vanity: for it took at least two months to get a suit made in those 'demob' days and few of us could get into our pre-war clothes."

Others were anxious, however, to graduate and make a beginning on their careers. "Every university has disquieting tales to tell about the first post-war session of 1919–20," J. Anderson Russell wrote. "The mood was different from that encountered a quarter of a century later in 1946. The uncertainty up to the last moment about whether we would win or lose, the overwhelming relief when we did win, the appalling casualties – seven million men of all nations killed – the cynicism that spread during the wrangles over the Peace Treaty, all these left their mark on the men who began their studies in the autumn of 1919. Most were too young to cling to futile hopes about the good old days ever coming back again. But they were very conscious that the decline in the pound's value to nine shillings and sixpence left them decidedly hard up.

"The older men who had interrupted their studies to go away to the war, had only one thought – to qualify as quickly as possible and to earn their livings. But the younger ones wanted to relax as well as to study. Never was there a session into which so many smokers, dances, dinners, theatre-nights, and cruises were crammed."

Principal Sir Donald MacAlister of Tarbert, Bt.

In the post-war sessions, the University was crammed from attic to cellars with students. In the session before the war, there had been 2,900 students. In the session that began in October 1919, there were 4,200. With so many more students packed into lecture rooms than could be comfortably accommodated, and with some of those students disposed to rowdiness, some classes got out of hand. "In one which I attended," J. Anderson Russell remembered, "the lecturer could not be heard above the continuous uproar, so he turned his back on the class and wrote his lecture on the blackboard. He did this doggedly twice a week from October to March."

EARLY in 1919, the question of a suitable University War Memorial was discussed by the Senate, the General Council, and the Students' Representative Council. A joint University War Memorial Committee was formed, representative of the teaching staff, students, the University Court, and the General Council.

1920-1930

AFTER THE CATERPILLAR

During the First World War, the number of students fell – in 1916 – to just over 1,600, most of them women. The 1920's were distinguished by the concerted efforts of both town and gown not merely to maintain but to improve the quality of teaching and research carried out by the University. Between 1921 and 1930 eight chairs were founded and a number of lectureships as well as four of the University's most important special lectureships, the Frazer, Macewen, Gibson, and David Murray lectureships.

But the decade began gaily with the first Students Charities Day. It was not an organised affair though a great deal of time was spent in decorating lorries and devising outlandish costumes. The prize for ingenuity was generally awarded to a curiously long caterpillar with a cloth-covered frame and at least twenty pairs of legs that perambulated the streets. When it was announced that the total amount collected was £4,000, there was some astonishment.

The experiment was repeated the following year. "A movie photographer spent much time at the march past in John Street," according to one eye-witness account, "posing the Lord Provost and other dignitaries in various groups for his newsreel but, when he was finished, it turned out that he was a student and that the roll in his camera was made of toilet paper. Sir Thomas Paxton (the Lord Provost) found this exploit less funny than the rest."

By 1927, the Charities Day takings had risen to £10,000 – including £3 in gold. The 1928 campaign was, however, one of the most enterprising

Students Charities Day. Early Version

of all. The slogan was "And a Penny". In another guise, moreover, it referred to – or so it was alleged – Miss Anne d'Apenny, the intrepid transatlantic swimmer whose progress across the Atlantic – harried by sharks, narrowly avoiding collisions with icebergs – was reported daily.

"When her arrival was announced for noon two days before Charities Day, an enormous crowd gathered. Conservative authorities put its size at ten thousand. Others guessed it to be nearer forty thousand. The Suspension Bridge became so crowded that it had to be cleared by the police. The resolute swimmer, actually a man from the University Swimming Club wearing a flaxen wig, slipped into the icy Clyde at George V Bridge, led by a rowing boat carrying a piper and restoratives, and swam under the Jamaica Street Bridge to land at the Great Clyde Street Wharf. Already blue with cold, he had a tremendous reception. . . ."

CHARITIES DAY did much in the twenties to dispel the traditional distrust of Town for Gown. In 1929, the Glasgow citizen still muttered, "Thae Students!" as he had done for generations and still does, but amiably and even appreciatively.

*A College Pudding author
at work on a comedy*

THE companion entertainment was College Pudding. It was not, to
begin with, a part of the Charities Day campaign but was held in
November in aid of S.R.C. funds. The name was, predictably, a gift to
those newspaper reporters instructed to write a review of it. "A most
appetising dish which should appeal to the palate of all epicures in
sparkling wit and clever inconsequential foolery," the *Glasgow Herald*
recorded in 1925. The puns were outrageous, the corps de ballet had
more hairy knees than elegance, and the jokes were largely incompre-
hensible to anyone outwith the range of the University chimes.

IN 1922, the students elected as their Rector, the Earl of Birkenhead
(F. E. Smith) whose rectorial address, delivered in November 1923,
produced at least one phrase that passed into common currency when
he spoke of the "glittering prizes" that the world offered "to stout
hearts and sharp swords". "A slight nervousness was perceptible in the
hurried opening sentences of his address," the *Glasgow Herald* reported,
"but it speedily passed and the remainder of his speech was given at an
even pace, the words clearly enunciated, and the phrases measured and

Lord Birkenhead delivers his rectorial address

Lord Birkenhead's rectorial installation

emphasised at appropriate points. From the beginning, the attention of his audience was gripped. . . ."

At the end of his tenure of office, Lord Birkenhead attended a farewell dinner in the Randolph Hall. He expressed his love and admiration of universities but added that the only chance he would ever have of being elected to a responsible position in any of them would be if the voting were left to the young.

On the day after his installation as Rector, the "great three-days bazaar organised with distinguished assistance by the students of Glasgow University to enable them to make effective appeal to the public for their welfare scheme was successfully inaugurated by the Viscountess Novar, under the chairmanship of the Lord Rector, the Earl of Birkenhead, and in the presence of a large company of distinguished citizens. . . . The result of their day's labours was the ingathering of a sum of £11,623 12s 2d."

"I was in charge of the Bazaar's Joy Town," C. A. Oakley wrote later, "and I saw little of the Lord Rector except for a fleeting visit. Throwing hoop-la rings was not his idea of fun and he did not linger in our vicinity."

Arrival of Sir Austen Chamberlain for rectorial installation

SIR Austen Chamberlain succeeded Lord Birkenhead as Rector and his arrival for his installation in November 1926 was awaited with some apprehension. His stiff manner, it was felt, might contrast unfavourably with his predecessor's informality. Accordingly, the instruction went out that everyone in the St Andrews Halls for the installation was to wear an eye glass in imitation of the Rector. Fifteen gross of monocles were sold in the Union beforehand. The Principal, Sir Donald MacAlister, further endeared himself to the students by wearing a monocle when he welcomed Sir Austen at the Central Station. And apart from Sir Austen himself, he was the only wearer of an eyeglass who knew how to keep it in place.

Stanley Baldwin, later Rector of the University, receiving the Freedom of the City of Glasgow in October 1925

THE apparent hold of the Conservative Party on the affections of Glasgow students continued with the election of Rector in 1928 of Stanley Baldwin: the vote of the women students, it was later estimated, played an important part in the election of both Chamberlain and Baldwin.

His campaign was enlivened indirectly by the appearance of Mrs Aimée Semple MacPherson who was invited to speak at a lunch-time meeting in the Union.

The evangelist arrived in the debating hall to find it strewn with the evidence of miss-spent youth in the shape of empty bottles, packs of cards, and overflowing ashtrays. Union officials did their best to cajole the audience to silence. At last, exasperated by their failure, she stepped forward and asked all those who wanted to listen to her to hold up their hands. The hands went up slowly but in the end, there was unanimity.

It is understood that, during the Vacation, members of the "Old Glasgow Club" are to make excavations on the unfinished Memorial Chapel to discover when the erection of this ancient building really commenced

DURING this decade, the welfare of the students assumed greater importance and was systematically organised by, notably, the establishment of the Student Welfare Committee. From it derived the impetus towards the improvement of the University's sporting, residential, and social amenities. The committee in turn derived much of its impetus from the energy and enthusiasm of the Principal, Sir Donald MacAlister.

In the summer of 1929, however, Sir Donald resigned the principalship. The Chancellor of the University, the Earl of Rosebery, had recently died and the General Council unanimously elected Sir Donald as Chancellor. As Principal he was succeeded by Professor Robert S. Rait of the Chair of Scottish History.

At the beginning of the twenties, construction began of a University Chapel on the western side of the Arts Quadrangle as a memorial to

those members of the University who fell in the First World War. It was designed by the firm of John Burnet, Son and Dick, architects. Progress in the building of it was slow and it was not dedicated until 1929.

A SIMPLER enterprise was that of a memorial to William Hunter whose benefactions created the great Hunterian Collections of the University. It was designed by Sir John J. Burnet and unveiled on Commemoration

Hunter Memorial

President Paderewski

Day, 1925, when it was discovered to be not the "nice, tall memorial" suggested by some of the students but rather a nice, wide memorial.

On that same Commemoration Day, one of the honorary graduands was the pianist and President of Poland, Paderewski. He gave a short recital in the Students' Union – two pieces by Chopin, a nocturne and minuet of his own composition. "When he had signified that the recital

Paderewski at the Students Union

was at an end," a report of the event reads, "the students rose to their feet and lustily declaimed 'Paderewski Ygorra'. There was an interesting lull while the press photographers posed Paderewski for a study at the piano in the course of which the famous pianist was heard to remark, 'Please don't ask me to smile'."

At the beginning of the decade, a memorial of an unofficial kind decorated the centre of the Medical Quadrangle. It was a laboratory, deplorable in appearance, which the Chemistry Department had been allowed to put there in 1919 on the understanding that it would be a

A gentleman from the Herald *informs Prof. Gibson that, owing to the amount of room taken up by his Degree results, it has been found necessary to curtail the Sports page*

temporary construction. The years passed: but no move was made to demolish it.

A group of engineering students decided that a lick of paint would help to advertise the eyesore. Late one night, accordingly, they set about decorating it. Lady MacAlister's dog seems to have been the first to detect their presence. The police were summoned for it was a period when the University was particularly apprehensive about the safety of the Hunterian Collections. Some of the painters escaped, one leaving the seat of his trousers on a railing spike in University Avenue. A few were caught and all eighteen students involved were fined £1 each by a not entirely unsympathetic Senate. The fine was paid by a collection in the classes.

AND the classes were large. In 1925, *G.U.M.* published a drawing in which "a gentleman from the *Glasgow Herald* informs Professor Gibson (of Mathematics) that, owing to the amount of room taken up by his Degree results, it has been found necessary to curtail the Sports page."

IN the Physiology classroom, Professor D. Noel Paton, the son of Sir Noel Paton, the painter, conducted experiments in the physiology of birds. "What happens to a duck's breathing when it is tail uppermost?" he asked. "The department was invaded by quantities of ducks and geese who should provide the answer", Professor R. C. Garry recalled. "They were housed in one of the odd open spaces or wells inside the building. Pandemonium reigned. For on a drowsy summer afternoon, with the windows wide open, a duck can punctuate most devastatingly and appositely the efforts of a lecturer to expound the transient verities of physiology."

D. Noel Paton

ANOTHER and more permanent form of pandemonium affecting the University was also suggested at this period, this time by the Corporation of Glasgow. A service of tramcars should, it was proposed, be run

The new Union

along University Avenue. The Court protested vigorously – and successfully.

At the very end of the decade, the Students' Union moved their headquarters from the crest of the hill to a new building at the end of University Avenue. "The building, which is constructed of stone, is designed in the Scottish baronial style. . . . The internal arrangements are of the most up-to-date description. . . . There will be a central heating system and the whole building is fitted for a vacuum system of cleaning so that," the reporter from the *Glasgow Herald* added hopefully, "all dust will be drawn through pipes by means of extraction fans to the basement."

The new building was opened on December 12th 1930 by the Rector, Mr Baldwin, with, among other observations, some comments on prigs. "The prig is a most terrible thing," he stated. "We all know a gentleman and we all know a prig and while we all like the one, the other never seems to meet with that general approval and sympathy which he feels he is entitled to. It always strikes me that in Glasgow it will be impossible for a prig to emerge. I think he would die and that is a very good thing."

86

1930-1940

HERR SKITLER'S WAR

UNIVERSITY OF GLASGOW

OPENING OF SESSION 1939-40

So far as can be foreseen at present, arrangements for the Beginning of Term will remain in force. ENROLMENT BEGINS ON MONDAY 2ND OCTOBER. CLASSES OPEN ON MONDAY 9TH OCTOBER.

(From the *Glasgow Herald* of September 6th 1939)

THE thirties began with depression and ended with war. They were not, however, as sombre a period as this would suggest. The growth of the University – in student numbers, in the numbers of chairs and subjects taught, in buildings, amenities, and in costs – continued. And cheerfulness was always breaking in as, for example, students debated the problem of women in trousers, and the emergence of the German politician with the Chaplin moustache whom they mocked as Herr Skitler.

IN 1931, jobs for graduates were hard to find. The records of the Appointments Committee reflect the difficulties that the graduate with his new degree faced. There was a decline in the number of vacancies notified to the committee and an increase in the number of registrations of graduates who had lost their posts. The period was, probably, the grimmest in the Committee's history. As regards women graduates, the

Herr Skitler – on Charities Day

slump produced a depressing procession of "the rejected asking what they can do". Student numbers continued to grow though, as Sir Hector Hetherington recalled later, one reason for the increase was the fact that "many could find no openings in the callings to which they would normally have gone".

By 1937, however, the secretary of the Committee was able to report an increase in the number of firms visiting the University and to note the keen demand for men with qualifications in Science and Engineering: Arts graduates who did not wish to teach remained a problem.

"WHAT Hollywood wears to-day, Q.M. Union wears to-morrow," the *Gilmorehill Globe* reflected sadly in 1933. "And the latest is trousers. . . . Please, Miss Gilmorehill, have some sense. DON'T DO IT! Stick to your frills. Imagine the Venus de Milo in flannels and think what Helen of Troy would have looked like in plus fours!"

"WHEN I went up to Gilmorehill for the first time," Jessie House wrote, "I wore a brown velvet coat with a blonde fur collar and a hat with a feather in it." Women students were no longer confined to Queen Margaret College and now had the freedom of Gilmorehill. "We Q. Emmas (the name had not long been invented and everybody thought it awfully clever) clung to Gilmorehill because of the opportunities it offered to become a Corporate Lifer. To be good Corporate Lifers was our ambition and we worked hard to achieve it."

She contributed to *G.U.M.* and her poem had been printed – "printed, what is more, in a special deep black border. It was, you must understand, an epitaph. Perhaps because we knew so little of death, we rather specialised in epitaphs, elegies, and similar sombre themes. In fact, we rather liked our poetry with a body in it."

THERE was elegiac material close to home for Q.M. students in the early 1930's for the old Queen Margaret College was abandoned and the buildings and grounds sold to the British Broadcasting Corporation. The increasing numbers of women students and new ordinances on the constitution of curricula combined to render impracticable the separate education of women within Glasgow University.

When, moreover, the men students moved in 1930 into their new Union building and left vacant their original Union, described by Stanley Baldwin as "that old rabbit-warren up the hill", the building was given to the Queen Margaret students. They gutted it, cleaned it, altered it, and generally transformed it to become the Queen Margaret Union.

That the building was not obtained without some guile on the part of the Q.M. students emerged during the opening ceremonies in February 1932. Principal Rait confessed that he had never quite "penetrated the mystery of an event which happened one summer day in 1929 when the Treasury Committee for Grants to Universities visited Glasgow. They went to the Queen Margaret College Union at eleven o'clock and they found the rooms absolutely packed full and students sitting in large numbers on the stairs. The president at that time assured him that nothing had been arranged and that it was just chance or providence which led the committee to choose eleven o'clock as the hour for their visit. . . . Whatever the explanation, the Treasury Committee impressed upon them (the University) the necessity of more accommodation for the Queen Margaret College Union."

In October 1932, the honorary degree of Doctor of Laws was conferred on the Duke and Duchess of York. "During the period the audience was assembling in the Bute Hall, where the graduation

Visit of the Duke and Duchess of York in October 1932

ceremony took place, the students made merry," the *Glasgow Herald* reported, "but their vocalism was more restrained than is customary upon ordinary occasions and they were singularly unresponsive when the University organist played "Ye Mariners of England", the song written by Thomas Campbell who was Lord Rector of the University for three terms and defeated Sir Walter Scott at the election in 1829. Popular melodies and parodies found greater favour. . . ."

Sir Daniel Stevenson

In January 1934, the Chancellor, Sir Donald MacAlister of Tarbert, Bt., died. He was succeeded by Sir Daniel Stevenson who observed in his address after his installation that since his election, he had been trying to find out what were his rights, duties, and privileges. Practically speaking, he discovered, the answer seemed to be "None". He proposed, however, to "get this ancient seat of learning brought as up-to-date as any in the Empire and leave to his successor something more than the mere sinecure with which his predecessors appeared to have been contented".

Two years later, Sir Hector Hetherington returned to Glasgow from Liverpool to be Principal in succession to Sir Robert Rait. "The bad years of depression had made a deep imprint upon both city and

University," he wrote later of his return. "Every department, especially in the Sciences, seemed to be woefully short of the space, staffing, and equipment that had been achieved by smaller and less famous universities elsewhere. But the men were here: and the deep springs of its ancient strength. About 1934, the tide had turned, new resources were flowing into the industries and commerce of the Clyde, and the Clyde was beginning to find means more adequate to its task. . . . If only Hitler had not interfered, the last ten years of the first five hundred might have seen some notable developments."

Return of Sir Hector Hetherington to Glasgow

SIR HECTOR and Lady Hetherington were greeted on their arrival in Glasgow by the President of the S.R.C., H. H. Munro, who expressed the wish that Lady Hetherington would find a place in the students' hearts second only to her husband.

"I wish it could be," Sir Hector replied. "But I will tell you something. My wife and I took our degrees on the same day. She got a first and I got a second."

LADY HETHERINGTON played an important part in improving the amenities of the University, notably in the planting of trees to commemorate the Coronation of King George VI and Queen Elizabeth.

92

When she planted the first of them, she had the assistance of a small boy with a seaside spade. In the three quadrangles, she planted or supervised the planting of 12 double cherries, 10 bird cherries, 4 geans, 24 birches, 3 weeping birches, 10 crab apples and, insurance against witchcraft, a rowan – some of which have survived.

On University Avenue, meanwhile, a more intractable problem relating to University amenities was beginning to manifest itself, In January

1937, the S.R.C. requested from the University Court increased parking facilities at Gilmorehill.

"University students have travelled a long way from the days of the country lad who arrived at the start of each term with a bag of meal," the *Glasgow Herald* informed its readers. "And they have done their travelling by motor car. . . . The daily motor show at the University must have been observed by passers-by and it has not remained unnoticed by the University authorities."

One of the University authorities made a wry appraisal of the situation. Professor Duncan Blair (of Anatomy) observed at a dinner of the

University's London Club that "if one saw a flourishing sports car, one would know that the driver was a student, and if one saw a decrepit thing of the pre-chromium era, they might be sure it belonged to the staff".

In another respect, students, women students in particular, had come a long way. In October 1937, the first woman Assessor was elected to the University Court. She was Miss Elizabeth Wallace, warden of Southpark House and she was elected by the General Council in "the quietest revolution that has ever happened in any institution".

In the same year, the students elected the pacifist Canon H. R. L. Sheppard as their Rector. Canon Sheppard nominated as his Assessor, the Rev. Dr George F. MacLeod, then minister of Govan Parish Church. The Rector died a few days after the election and another election, in which Dr MacLeod was one of the candidates, was held. Sir Archibald Sinclair was elected.

On September 3rd 1939 war was declared. The seriousness of the situation was brought home to the citizens of Glasgow in the following month by the silencing of the University chimes. This decision of the Chief Constable provoked energetic protests. No one, it was argued, could possibly mistake the bells for an air-raid warning and now that all sirens and hooters had ceased, the chimes were more necessary than ever to the regulation of the occupations of those within earshot. The protests were effective. At the beginning of November, the Chief Constable informed the University authorities that "under the recent Control of Noise Order, the Scottish Home Department has withdrawn the prohibition on the ringing of the great bell of the University". The great bell rang again, as usual, on November 8th.

In the middle of November, the first wartime graduation was held when a number of the graduands wore khaki or air force blue uniforms under their gowns. An unusually large number of degrees were conferred *in absentia*. On the following day, the new Reading Room in University Avenue was opened.

Towards the end of 1939, fierce debate was aroused at least – in the columns of *G.U.M.,* which continued to appear – over the decision of the S.R.C. to hold a Charities Day in 1940. "There is a quixotry in this

94

Reading Room

desperate disregard of circumstances which is almost admirable," the
G.U.M. editorial criticised. Charities Day, it went on, had declined from
the brave days of the early thirties. "Glasgow is tired of us and we may
as well face up to the fact."

Undeterred, the S.R.C. pressed on and the Charities Day was held on
April 27th 1940 when £8000 was raised, a sum which *G.U.M.* was
compelled to concede, represented "a very creditable piece of work

under existing conditions and a far greater return than might well have been expected".

FOR enemy aircraft, the University buildings were an admirable landmark. In November 1940, concern for the University's cultural and scientific collections provoked an appeal for volunteer guards to form a Volunteer Fire Service. There was no difficulty about finding volunteers from staff and students.

1940-1950

TASKS ESSENTIAL TO THE RESTORING OF ORDER

"THE University has weathered the war surprisingly well," the Principal, Sir Hector Hetherington, wrote in August 1946 in one of his famous letters to graduates. "It has, of course, lost ground. As regards our material equipment, we shall take some years to get back even to pre-war standards, and considerably longer to reach the standard which, but for the war, we should now have attained. The University has to face the heavy tasks of the immediate future under formidable handicaps; and these are all the harder to put up with since at this very time we want to offer to the men and women returning from the Services the fullest possible opportunity to make good the training they have lost."

A WARTIME editorial in *G.U.M.* took a blacker view of the situation. "There is a very definite risk that the salt which made University life so sweet before the war may not be available again for so long after the war that the taste of University life as it should be will have passed from memory. There is no tradition so ancient and famous and yet so frail as that of the corporate life."

The demands of national service, at a variety of levels, took precedence over those of corporate life. In January 1941, the University of Glasgow formed the first University Air Squadron. In the 1942–43 session, the After-Blitz Corps was commended to students as a form of national service. "In volunteering, a student undertakes to attend at the University on the morning following a blitz," *G.U.M.* announced, "when he or she will be directed to some task essential to the restoring

Visit of General de Gaulle in June 1942

of order in the area which has been attacked. The work may be demolition, first-aid, canteen work, or form-filling – each student will be allotted the task most suitable for him or her."

In the spring of 1944, the *Glasgow Herald* carried the announcement that "Scottish students are being asked to volunteer for transport duties when the Second Front opens. Regional transport pools are being formed in Glasgow and Edinburgh. . . . The (Scottish National) Union of Students had decided that the best use could be made of their 7,000–8,000 members by the Ministry of Labour's directing them to essential work during the summer months. After discussion, however, it was decided to use every available student for transport duties from June to mid-August when a transfer would be made to harvesting. Full details of the wages to be paid for transport work are not yet available but it is stated that the rates will be higher than those already fixed for harvesting which are 58s a week for men students and 41s for women."

DISTINGUISHED visitors to the University from the Allies included President Benes of Czechoslovakia and in June 1942 General de Gaulle. In November of the same year, Hero of the Soviet Union Senior Lieutenant Vladimir Pchelintsev visited the Students' Union in Glasgow. "He was ecstatic with delight," it was reported, "as he paraded the platform of the Union wearing a red undergraduate gown over his Red Army uniform."

THE suspension (temporary as it turned out) of the University chimes in the autumn of 1939 had seemed ominous at the time. The war years brought with them the suspension of another institution that was, for so ancient a foundation, even more serious. The University Calendar ceased publication with the issue of 1940–1941 and did not resume until the 1947–48 session.

AT the beginning of the 1943–44 session, the number on the University roll was 3,200 students and the Principal expressed himself as a little alarmed at the increased pressure for admission to the University, "particularly by rather young women."

IN one respect, the 1940's were vintage years. A stream of distinguished poets, authors, and historians beat a path to Glasgow to deliver the David Murray and W. P. Ker lectures. The David Murray lecturers included D. W. Brogan on American Federalism, V. H. Galbraith on Matthew Paris, R. W. Chapman on Johnsonian scholarship, David Douglas on the historians of the Norman Conquest, and F. L. Ganshof on the coronation of Charlemagne.

The Ker lecturers were, if anything, an even more dazzling assembly: T. S. Eliot on "The Music of Poetry", Lord David Cecil on "Antony and Cleopatra", E. M. Forster on "The Development of English Prose between 1918 and 1939", Charles Morgan on "The Artist in the Community", Edwin Muir on "The Politics of King Lear", and Helen Waddell on "Poetry in the Dark Ages".

THE University celebrated the end of the Second World War with a Grand Victory Ball in the Bute Hall. The account of it in *G.U.M.* suggests the turn of the century rather than the mid 1940's. In the upper reaches of the hall, apparently, "there poured forth the ringing laughter of the youth and maidens, nimbly playing at Hunt the Slipper among the organ pipes. And who can say what manly junior lecturer gazed long into the adoring eyes of his Junior Honours student, till suddenly he snatched her in his arms and bore her forth, as Porphyro bore his Madeline, up the twisting turreted staircase to the lofty eminence of the tower."

IN October 1945, the first rectorial election since 1938 was held. The candidates were Sir John Boyd Orr, Lord Lovat, and Sir Thomas Beecham the last of whom afforded a splendid opportunity to parodists ("Hark the herald angels sing, / Beecham's pills are just the thing"). Sir John was elected by a substantial majority: his term of office was, however, short. In the following year he was elected Chancellor of the University.

IN 1946, a refectory was established in the University "to provide cheap meals," G.U.M. reported, "for those who do not mess at the Union. . . . Besides purveying good plain British cooking between the hours of twelve and three daily, the refectory provides an opportunity for the ambitious maiden to discover how much her beau ideal can do with a knife and fork before proceeding to entrap him in any semi-permanent sort of snare. In addition you pay for your food with nice wee tiddly-winks and the place is called not canteen or even cafeteria, but refectory which is enough to double prices all round.

"We are intrigued to observe that this new institution occupies the premises which were known many years ago as the Dressing Station, in the days when it housed one of the more notorious of the old fireguard pickets."

SOLDIERS, sailors, and airmen recognisable in their "demob" suits returned to resume or begin their studies. Some – like their predecessors after the First World War – were anxious to complete their courses and start earning a living for themselves and their families. Some were impatient of the discipline of lectures and examinations and of the company of the "children", the students up from school, with whom they found themselves. They said so, and in a few cases, left.

One ex-service student recalled that on his return "Sir Hector Hetherington looked older as indeed did most of the staff for the strain of the war years had taken its toll. Somehow the vast gulf that separates the ordinary student from his Principal had narrowed and many of us recalled with gratitude that during the war on any occasion for rejoicing or sorrowing, the first letter was usually from Sir Hector. It meant much

Sir John Boyd Orr in carriage drawn by "Blues" in February 1947

Sir John Boyd Orr delivers his rectorial address

– There's oor Wullie!   – Hoo d'ye ken?   – By 'is splay feet

to us. It says much, too, for his office staff who must have meticulously examined each casualty and honours list."

Post-war "College Puddings" were of a different character from those of earlier years. For one thing, that of January 1946 made a profit of £500: entertainment-starved Glaswegians booked 3000 seats beforehand in the theatre. This particular show was, moreover, closely linked to Charities Week and was clearly no longer a private University venture.

And while it was not, of course, a University enterprise nor a

"College Pudding", the apotheosis of student entertainments was achieved in 1949 when James Bridie wrote "The Tintock Cup" for the Citizens' Theatre.

Meanwhile, on Gilmorehill, the Principal looked ahead. "Just before the war, Glasgow had rather over 4000 students, in most departments too heavy a load (i.e. too heavy in the interests of the students themselves) both for the accommodation and for the available staff," he wrote in 1946. "We should have preferred not to increase our student numbers but to concentrate on bringing up our resources to the point at which we could have done more for the students already here. But that course would have denied the chance of a University education to some students and to some classes of students who in the national interest ought to have that chance. We expect therefore gradually to increase to a normal student enrolment of about 5000. . . . But we cannot accomplish this without large additions to the already large building programme on which we had embarked, to meet our ordinary needs before the war. Graduates who live in or near Glasgow have seen the first instalment of that programme in the new Chemistry building and in the new Reading Room. That is a relatively small fraction of what will have to be undertaken in the next two years".

1950-1960

FIVE HUNDRED YEARS ON

"Now that it has come and gone, the 'Fifth Centenary' may appear to most of us to have been inevitable. It is not perhaps sufficiently realised how near we were, but for the wise counsels of the original committee in 1948, to having a Demi-Millenary, Quincentenary, Quingentenary, Quingenary, Tenth Jubilee, Hundredth Lustre, or even merely a Five Hundredth Anniversary."

THE decision having been taken as to what the University were to celebrate in 1951, the complex arrangements whereby the University would, in the company of distinguished guests from home and abroad, mark its five hundredth birthday, were made. The committee on whose shoulders devolved most of the responsibility began work well before the year of anniversary. The climax of the celebrations was the week beginning June 18th 1951.

"As to the June affairs, now that it is over, we may admit we had our qualms. We had to receive 300 delegates (+ wives) from Universities and Academies the world over, to arrange their entertainment, to get them and their robes to the right places at the right times, marshal them and steer them and ourselves through the ritual of the ceremonies," Sir Hector Hetherington wrote, in the comparative peace of the month of September 1951.

"We had to plan for the reception of many hundreds of our graduates – many of them from far, distant places – and other official guests: and to organise an elaborate system of traffic control. For us amateurs at such a game, it was a formidable job: and up to the morning of June 19th when we staged the first of the three major acts, we had our

Torch-bearers for the Fifth Centenary

doubts. But that went beautifully: and from then on we were on top of the world. In my time, I have seen many high academic festivals. But the Glasgow Fifth Centenary was the finest of them all."

THERE was one major disappointment. The illness of the King prevented his visit and that of the Queen and Princess Margaret. "Our celebration," the Principal commented, "was shorn of its most brilliant element."

Lord Macmillan delivers the Commemorative oration, June 1951

AFTER three days of formal celebration (the presentation of Addresses, the service in Glasgow Cathedral, the honorary graduation, Lord Macmillan's commemorative address, lunches, dinners, receptions) the week ended with "a day of pure holiday on Friday, June 22nd. We had chartered a steamer for the day and at 10 a.m. embarked, 800 strong at the Bridge Wharf." The University's guests were enchanted by the sail and the scenery. One of the most eminent said as he stepped ashore at Wemyss Bay: "Well, it is clear that you are the masters of the earth and have a strong pull in heaven."

THE week did, however, present some difficulties as J. B. Neilson, secretary of the Fifth Centenary Committee remembered. "The issue of invitations to all our honorary graduates had presented unexpected problems," he wrote, "but in this difficulty we had been much aided by the recollections of members of the committee, by reference to *Who's Who* and *Who Was Who*, and, in the last resort, to our own unofficial compilation *"Who Might Be Who"*. The latter was not always infallible and it is perhaps a matter for congratulation that our mail brought only a few such expressions of polite astonishment as those received from a prominent citizen of the Free State and a pastoralist in New South Wales on whom we had inadvertently conferred Honorary Doctorates."

French delegation to Fifth Centenary celebrations

"The volume of correspondence from members of the General Council was a swelling tribute of loyalty to their Alma Mater which necessitated expansion of office space and staff. Applications for some 10,000 tickets were received. . . . This number would, we believe, have been much higher but for the earnest pre-occupations which, unfortunately, leave many graduates little time to open the envelopes of the half-yearly General Council papers."

INEVITABLY, there were some complaints – from, for example, a married woman graduate impatient of the restrictions the committee had to impose on account of the overwhelming number of requests for tickets. "It appears," she wrote, "that had I been single, I could have brought a friend but now I can bring only my husband."

And mishaps such as that which befell the delegate who appealed to the committee: "I have lost my wife. If you find her, please keep her."

And misunderstandings such as, presumably, that of the distinguished delegate of the Soviet Academy of Sciences who turned up during the week after the main celebrations. "He had been unable," Sir Hector recorded, "to reach Glasgow before that day. But his visit extended over two pleasant days and we were happy to receive the greetings of the academy."

Lady Hetherington opens the Memorial Gates

ALTHOUGH the Fifth Centenary celebrations constituted a landmark for 1951 and, indeed, for the decade as a whole, other events ensured the University of Glasgow a place in the headlines. It was the decade of the rowdy rectorials which began with the installation of Dr John Mac-Cormick in St Andrews Halls amid a barrage of missiles and a constant din of cheers and jeers.

Dr T. J. Honeyman, who succeeded him, received gentler treatment when he was installed in October 1954. "Advocates of comparative decorum," the *Glasgow Herald* reported, "won a handsome victory on points."

It was the installation of Mr R. A. (now Lord) Butler in February 1958 which altered the pattern of subsequent ceremonies. The miserable

108

Installation as rector of Mr John McCormick

Dr Honeyman delivers his rectorial address

Mr R. A. Butler's installation as rector

display of "witless student antics" drew down on Glasgow students the indignation and disapproval of their fellow citizens. The Rector himself claimed, politely, to "have enjoyed it. I just think you have to put up with it. It did not worry me at all," he said. "I am used to trouble in the House of Commons."

MORE constructively, the 1950's saw the beginning of the massive building programme that was to continue through the 1960's. Notable additions to the landscape of Gilmorehill were the Engineering South building, the Modern Languages Building, and the Physical Education (Stevenson) Building.

The changes in the nature of the University wrought by its physical extension were foreshadowed at the time of the Fifth Centenary celebrations by Walter Elliot. "The first thing to remember in the comparison between Then (the years before the First World War) and Now is that the bigger the University, the greater the danger to its soul. The next is that leisure is the key to understanding and that leisure must be regained by hook or by crook. And the last and greatest is that there are as good fish in the sea as ever came out of it."

A SERIOUS loss which affected the whole city was the abolition of tramcars. On Gilmorehill, there was mourning for the loss of the University tram. "I suppose in these days (1951) when the streets are stuffed with motors, the tram like the old soldier was bound to fade away," the Principal lamented. "But I always had a quiet hope that at least the University tram would last my time. . . . Of course, the Glasgow trams have never been quite the same since they took to announcing their route by number rather than by colour. The white car for the University, green for Anniesland or Parkhead, red for the long line of Dumbarton Road, yellow for Cathcart, and blue for your occasional venture to the independence of Rutherglen. No doubt there were points of complication: but by and large you knew where you were in those days and didn't have to carry a kind of mathematical table in your head . . . the bus routes are now a pattern of mystery and we say hard things about them."

WITH the middle fifties, the University – like other institutions of the kind – reached a watershed in its development. There was a sense in which the Old College, assumed to have died with the nineteenth century, survived into the second quarter of the twentieth: the pre-1939 University bore, arguably, a closer resemblance to the College of 1870 than to the University of 1970.

The University became news. Headlines of the order of "Need for University Expansion", "Increased Grants to Universities", "University Entry Standards – Objections to Proposed New Regulations", "Universities Behind the Times?" and "Law Degree Change Criticised" (this last provoked a furious controversy) proliferated. And, possibly, one of the most significant headlines of all concerned – in February 1959 – the first computer to be installed in a Scottish University, at Glasgow. "Computer does 10,000 additions in second," was the headline.

AT the end of the decade, deterioration set in – fortunately it was a temporary aberration – in the presentation of the University's coat of arms on blazer badges. For some reason, the separate components of it shrank so that in the succinct description of the Clerk of Senate, Professor C. J. Fordyce: "The mace has relapsed into a crowned spurtle; the surmounting salmon has dwindled into a detached minnow."

1960-1970

NO COMPLETION, NO FINALITY

"Ye walls that massive rise on Gilmorehill,
   With stately tower and many a turret crowned,
   Soon shall the thronging youth thy precincts fill,
   Soon render thine environs classic ground".

AND behold, the half was not told to Mr Sinclair, rhyming his eulogy of the new University buildings on Gilmorehill in the 1870's. The classic ground now extends over a large part of Hillhead. Towers there are still: the austere lines of the new library now balance Gilbert Scott's Gothic-though there is a perceptible shortage of turrets.

THE 1960's have seen the University expand in every direction and at a speed unparalleled by any event in the previous five centuries of its history. Nearly 30 appointments were made to new chairs in subjects ranging from Fine Art and Architecture to Medical Cardiology and Town and Regional Planning. In April 1961, the Principal, Sir Hector Hetherington, expected the number of students to rise from 5,500 to about 6,500 at the end of the decade. He added, at the time, that he could not see how the University could expand on its present site beyond a target of 6,500 students. At June 15th 1969, the number of students was 8,881.

The new buildings erected constitute, virtually, a second University on the north side of University Avenue. There are the headquarters of the Social Sciences (in the Adam Smith building), Mathematics, and, part of Engineering and the Basic Science building is within sight of completion. At the bottom of Church Street are the Virology and Genetics buildings. At Garscube, the Faculty of Veterinary Science is, largely, accommodated and there too is the new University Observatory.

Amenity buildings include the new Refectory and the Queen Margaret Union, again north of University Avenue. And probably the most notable addition of all to the city skyline is the new library building.

THE decade of expansion began, however, with the retirement of the man who launched it, Sir Hector Hetherington. Sadly, he did not live to see some of the new projects completed: he died in January 1965.

Asked what would be the most urgent problems he would hand over to his successor, he replied: "He will have plenty of vexations and urgent problems over the site and its physical development. We need more room to provide better social and tutorial facilities, and for research. . . . Nearly every week some new proposal – perfectly sound – is put up for some new line of research which would require more room."

The problems devolved upon Dr Charles H. Wilson who returned to

Portrait of Sir Hector Hetherington

Sir Charles Wilson, Principal of the University, 1961

Glasgow from the University of Leicester where he had been vice-chancellor. Professor D. W. Brogan commented that "after the long and memorable consulship of Sir Hector Hetherington, it will be a difficult job to succeed".

WHILE the University of Glasgow expanded on Gilmorehill and at Garscube, one long-standing tie was cut in 1963 when the Royal

College of Science and Technology became the University of Strathclyde. A new name for the old "Tec" was not, when it came to the bit, easy to find and suggestions included the St Mungo University, the Royal Scottish Institution of Technology, the University of Clydeside, and Anderson's University; the last commemorative, of course, of the litigious Professor of Natural Philosophy in the parent University whose will set the events in train that eventually produced the University of Strathclyde.

THE successor to Mr Butler as Rector of the University was Lord Hailsham who was installed in a ceremony in the Bute Hall of the University. In October 1962, the students elected as his successor Mr Albert Lutuli, the Nobel Peace Prize winner who was never allowed, however, by the South African Government to travel to Glasgow for his installation.

IN March 1962, the Department of Biochemistry ensured their place in University history by going on strike – for an hour. This was, it was

Charities Day – later version

Charities Day

claimed, the first time in the history of Glasgow and possibly in the history of any University, that such extreme action had been taken. The cause was dissatisfaction with Government policy on University grants and Government treatment of salary claims.

THE increase in the number of students throughout the sixties placed fresh burdens on the teaching staff of the University. In 1965, they acquired a new tool in the shape of the Television Service which was established in Southpark House.

THE same increase in student numbers created difficulties in the field of staff-student relations and it was with the object of improving communications between the two bodies that a staff-student committee was formed by the Senate in 1966.

Within the same field, the Universities (Scotland) Act of 1966 made provision for the drawing up of codes of discipline and for the first time in the University's history, the University Court, on the recommendation of the Senate, formulated such a code in 1967.

WHILE the character of student unruliness altered throughout the university world in the 1960's, the Engineering students at Glasgow adhered to tradition – at least during the Charities Week of 1964. The statues in George Square, it was decided, would be none the worse of being brightened up with some paint. The effect was not the same as when their predecessors painted the Chemistry Laboratory in the Medical quadrangle in the 1920's: the statues are still there.

Drawing by Muirhead Bone of Glasgow University from Cessnock Dock

It was during the late 1960's, moreover, that Professor Stanley Nisbet of the Department of Education, and Miss Barbara L. Napier, Senior Tutor to Women Students, carried out a survey of the origins and progress of students in the University. They thought before they began, Professor Nisbet wrote of the survey, that they knew a lot about students: what they learned was how much they still had to discover. Especially about the student who in answer to a questionnaire, wrote: "When I first went to University, I had no moral sense. I acquired moral sense but was then unable to pass examinations."

"I USED to think that I might hand over a nice tidy table to my successor," Sir Hector Hetherington said when he retired in 1961,